Virginia Real Estate Wholesaling Residential Real Estate Investor & Commercial Real Estate Investing

Learn to Buy Real Estate Finance & Find

Wholesale Real Estate Houses in Virginia

by

Brian Mahoney

Get Our Video Training Program at:

(Zero Cost Internet Marketing complete 142 video series)

https://goo.gl/UFSIY6

http://www.BrianSMahoney.com

ABOUT THE AUTHOR

Brian Mahoney is the author of over 100 business start-up guides, real estate investing programs and Christian literature. He started his company MahoneyProducts in 1992.

He served in the US Army and worked over a decade for the US Postal Service. An active real estate investor, he has also served as a minister for the Churches of Christ in Virginia and Michigan.

He has degree's in Business Administration and Applied Science & Computer Programming.

His books and video training programs have helped thousands of people all over the world start there own successful business.

http://www.briansmahoney.com/

Copyright © 2017 Brian Mahoney
All rights reserved.

DEDICATION

This book is dedicated to my son's
Christian and Matthew.
A blessing from God and the joy of my life.

ACKNOWLEDGMENTS

I WOULD LIKE TO ACKNOWLEDGE ALL THE HARD WORK OF THE MEN AND WOMEN OF THE UNITED STATES MILITARY, WHO RISK THEIR LIVES ON A DAILY BASIS, TO MAKE THE WORLD A SAFER PLACE.

Disclaimer

This book was written as a guide to starting a business. As with any other high yielding action, starting a business has a certain degree of risk. This book is not meant to take the place of accounting, legal, financial or other professional advice. If advice is needed in any of these fields, you are advised to seek the services of a professional.

While the author has attempted to make the information in this book as accurate as possible, no guarantee is given as to the accuracy or currency of any individual item. Laws and procedures related to business are constantly changing.

Therefore, in no event shall Brian Mahoney, the author of this book be liable for any special, indirect, or consequential damages or any damages whatsoever in connection with the use of the information herein provided.

All Rights Reserved

No part of this book may be used or reproduced in any manner whatsoever without the written permission of the author.

Table of Contents

Chapter 1: **Real Estate Wholesaling**

How to Find Wholesale Residential & Commercial Real Estate

Chapter 2: Finding Real Estate in Virginia

Quick & Easy: Virginia's Wholesale Properties

Chapter 3: **Financing Real Estate**

8 Realistic Ways to Finance Real Estate

Chapter 4: **Small Business Grants**

How to write a Winning Grant Proposal

Chapter 5: **How to Buy a House**

Strategies to Making Your Offer

Chapter 6: **For Sale By Owner**

12 Steps to Selling Any Investment Property Fast!

Chapter 7: **Millionaire Rolodex**

Get Started Fast with these Business Web Sites!

Chapter 8: **Billionaire Business Advice**

When they talk, we listen.

CHAPTER 1
REAL ESTATE WHOLESALING

How to Fine Wholesale Residential & Commercial Real Estate

How To Find Wholesale Real Estate

There are several basic methods to find real estate at wholesale prices. There are foreclosures and pre foreclosures, so get excited! There are hundreds of great deals just waiting for you to find them! The first method is Searching Public Records.

Searching Public Records

Go to your county's recorders office and look for notice of default or notice of sale. The advantage of this method is that many newly posted properties have not been seen by your competition. The disadvantage is that it usually takes more time to find property than the other methods.

Here is a tip. When ever a county clerk helps you, get that person's name and thank them face to face. Then go home and call the office and thank them again. Wait about a week. Then purchase a thank you card and mail it. Your kindness is going to stand out to that clerk. In turn that clerk is not likely to forget you. You in turn will likely have an ally in that office. The old saying "It's not what you know, but who you know." This method helps the clerk and yourself get to know each other quicker than usual. At the very least, you should feel good for being a nice person!

How To Find Wholesale Real Estate

Another advantage to searching public records is Probate Properties. You will need to be educated in your local area's probate laws to purchase those properties.

Probate is required for all estates that are not protected by a trust. The average duration of probate is 7 to 8 months.

If the house is owned outright, the estate is responsible for remitting property taxes and insurance premiums throughout the probate process.

Estate administrators can elect to sell the property if it is causing financial harm to the estate. If the estate does not have sufficient funds to cover outstanding debts, the probate judge can order the property sold.

How a probate house is sold depends on the type of probate that is used. "Court Confirmation" is the most common type of probate used. A judge must approve all of the aspects of the management of the estate. Independent Administration of Estate's Act (IAEA) governs the 2nd type of probate administration. It allows estate executors to engage in estate administrative affairs without the court management.

How To Find Wholesale Real Estate

To purchase probate property you have to know which probate system is being applied. Properties can be bought directly from the estate executor when Independent Administration of Estate's process is in effect. You can place your bid through the court system when court approval is required.

An investor interested in finding probate real estate must research public records. When people pass away their last will and testament is recorded in the probate court. The last will and testament will contain valuable information such as the estate assets, who is the beneficiary, and contact info for whoever is administrating for the estate.

Property records should show if there are any liens on the property and if so, who holds the lien. They should also show the properties appraised value, the year it was constructed, the square footage and the lot size. The records may also help you to determine if there have been any tax liens placed on the property.

Do your due diligence when purchasing any type of real estate. Bring in professional help in the form of building inspectors, lawyers and any other professionals that can help protect you when needed.

How To Find Wholesale Real Estate

Using the Internet

I will provide you with a Small Real Estate Rolodex of web sites later in this chapter. Many are completely free and have tons of information. One success algorithm for buying a property is that you should never, never, purchase one property without looking at, at least 100 other properties. Being able to search online makes using this formula very easy.

Using Local Papers and Journals

Local papers and journals. By law many foreclosures have to be posted in the local paper. This can mean a goldmine of opportunity for you. With newspaper circulation in decline, many people are simply not looking in the newspaper anymore. Advantage you.

Next I am going to cover several categories of real estate sources.

* **Nationwide banks & Foreclosure Properties**

* **Government Foreclosure Properties**

* **Commercial Real Estate**

* **FSBO - For Sale By Owner**

How To Find Wholesale Real Estate

Nationwide Banks & Foreclosure Properties

Bank of America

http://foreclosures.bankofamerica.com/

I have purchased property using this web site. It is my favorite because they have a large nationwide inventory and their web site is easy to navigate and sort properties.

Wells Fargo

https://reo.wellsfargo.com/

I placed myself on their mailing list, and get property updates on a monthly basis.

Ocwen Financial Corporation

http://www.ocwen.com/reo

Founded in 1988 they are one of the largest mortgage companies in America.

How To Find Wholesale Real Estate

Hubzu

http://www.hubzu.com/

Hubzu is a nationwide real estate auction web site. Very easy to use. This is a great web site for comparing property prices nationwide.

How To Find Wholesale Real Estate

Government Foreclosure Properties

One advantage purchasing from the government is that there is no emotional attachment to the property. Don't be afraid to make a offer that is lower than the listed price. I once argued with a real estate agent who refused to place a offer lower than the stated price. Eventually I got him to place the offer. (Remember that they work for you, however some government properties can't be purchased unless you go through a HUD or government approved agent.) It was countered twice, before I decided to purchase another property. But they countered with two offers lower than the listed price.

If you are reading a ebook version of this book then you should be able to access these web sites by clicking the links below. Buy if you are reading a paperback version of this book then be careful when looking for government properties. There are many web sites pretending to be government web sites and some will attempt to charge you fees for information about government properties.

How To Find Wholesale Real Estate Government Foreclosure Properties

Fannie Mae
The Federal National Mortgage Association

https://www.fanniemae.com/singlefamily/reo-vendors

Department of Housing and Urban Development

https://www.hudhomestore.com/Home/Index.aspx

The Federal Deposit Insurance Corporation

https://www.fdic.gov/buying/owned/

The **United States Department of Agriculture**

https://properties.sc.egov.usda.gov/resales/index.jsp

United States Marshals

https://www.usmarshals.gov/assets/sales.htm#real_estate

How To Find Wholesale Real Estate Commercial Real Estate Properties

City Feet

is a nationwide database of Commercial Real Estate Property

http://www.cityfeet.com/#

The Commercial Real Estate Listing Service

is a nationwide database of Commercial Real Estate Property

https://www.cimls.com/

Land . Net

is a nationwide database of land, commercial real estate for sale and for lease.

http://www.land.net/

Loop . Net

is a nationwide database of Commercial Real Estate Property

http://www.loopnet.com/

How To Find Wholesale Real Estate

FSBO – For Sale By Owner

By Owner

http://www.byowner.com/

For sale by owner in Canada

http://www.fsbo-bc.com/

For sale by owner Central

http://www.fsbocentral.com/

For sale by Owner: world's largest FSBO web site

http://www.forsalebyowner.com/

Ranch by owner

http://www.ranchbyowner.com/

Chapter 2
Finding Real Estate in Virginia

**Quick & Easy Access to
Virginia's Wholesale Properties**

Getting Started

When Investing in Virginia first you have to determine what county you want to purchase in. To help you decide, below is a list of all counties in Virginia with their population and square miles. After the list of all the counties, you get a Goldmine Rolodex of web site address of Wholesale Government Tax Sale Properties and More!

VA Counties	Population	Square Miles
Fairfax County	1,142,234	396
Prince William County	451,721	338
Loudoun County	375,629	520
Chesterfield County	335,687	426
Henrico County	325,155	238
Arlington County	229,164	26
Stafford County	142,003	270
Spotsylvania County	130,475	401
Albemarle County	105,703	723
Hanover County	103,227	473
Montgomery County	97,653	388
Roanoke County	94,409	251

VA Counties	Population	Square Miles
Frederick County	83,199	415
Rockingham County	78,593	851
Bedford County	77,724	755
Augusta County	74,314	971
James City County	73,147	143
Fauquier County	68,782	650
York County	67,837	106
Pittsylvania County	62,194	978
Franklin County	56,264	692
Campbell County	55,086	504
Washington County	54,591	564
Henry County	51,881	382
Culpeper County	49,432	381
Shenandoah County	43,190	512
Tazewell County	42,899	520
Wise County	39,718	403
Warren County	39,083	214

VA Counties	Population	Square Miles
Prince George County	37,862	266
Gloucester County	37,143	217
Isle of Wight County	36,314	316
Orange County	35,385	342
Halifax County	35,125	814
Louisa County	34,602	498
Pulaski County	34,332	321
Botetourt County	33,347	543
Accomack County	32,973	455
Amherst County	31,914	475
Smyth County	31,470	452
Mecklenburg County	31,081	624
Caroline County	29,984	533
Carroll County	29,724	476
Wythe County	29,119	463
Powhatan County	28,031	261
Russell County	27,891	475

VA Counties	Population	Square Miles
Dinwiddie County	27,852	504
Fluvanna County	26,235	287
King George County	25,515	180
Lee County	24,742	437
Page County	23,726	311
Prince Edward County	22,952	353
Buchanan County	22,776	504
Rockbridge County	22,354	600
Goochland County	22,253	284
Scott County	22,126	537
New Kent County	20,392	210
Greene County	19,162	157
Southampton County	18,109	600
Patrick County	18,045	483
Westmoreland County	17,629	229
Buckingham County	17,032	581
Giles County	16,708	358

VA Counties	Population	Square Miles
Brunswick County	16,698	566
King William County	16,269	275
Grayson County	16,012	443
Alleghany County	15,677	446
Nottoway County	15,673	315
Floyd County	15,651	382
Appomattox County	15,414	334
Dickenson County	15,115	333
Nelson County	14,785	472
Clarke County	14,363	177
Madison County	13,134	322
Amelia County	12,903	357
Lunenburg County	12,299	432
Northumberland County	12,232	192
Charlotte County	12,201	475
Northampton County	12,155	207
Greensville County	11,885	296

VA Counties	Population	Square Miles
Sussex County	11,715	491
Essex County	11,130	258
Lancaster County	10,965	133
Middlesex County	10,606	130
Cumberland County	9,719	298
Richmond County	8,908	192
Mathews County	8,862	86
Rappahannock County	7,378	267
King and Queen County	7,158	316
Charles City County	7,040	182
Surry County	6,709	279
Bland County	6,561	359
Craig County	5,211	330
Bath County	4,470	532
Highland County	2,214	416

VA Cites	Population	Square Miles
City of Alexandria	147,391	15
City of Bristol	17,367	12
City of Buena Vista	6,349	7
City of Charlottesville	45,049	10
City of Chesapeake	222,209	341
City of Colonial Heights	16,897	8
City of Covington	6,303	4
City of Danville	48,411	43
City of Emporia	5,665	7
City of Fairfax	21,498	6
City of Falls Church	12,332	2
City of Franklin	8,346	8
City of Fredericksburg	24,286	10
City of Galax	6,837	8
City of Hampton	146,437	52
City of Harrisonburg	40,468	18
City of Hopewell	22,354	10

VA Cites	Population	Square Miles
City of Lexington	6,867	2
City of Lynchburg	65,269	49
City of Manassas	40,605	10
City of Manassas Park	14,273	2
City of Martinsville	15,416	11
City of Newport News	180,726	68
City of Norfolk	245,782	54
City of Norton	3,904	7
City of Petersburg	33,740	23
City of Poquoson	11,566	16
City of Portsmouth	96,470	33
City of Radford	15,859	10
City of Richmond	210,309	60
City of Roanoke	94,911	43
City of Salem	24,747	15
City of Staunton	23,853	20
City of Suffolk	63,677	400

VA Cites	Population	Square Miles
City of Virginia Beach	447,021	248
City of Waynesboro	19,520	14
City of Williamsburg	14,068	9
City of Winchester	23,585	9

Virginia is a Tax Deed state.

As of the writting of this book, all of these websites are up and running. From time to time some will change their address. If a site does not come up sometimes using the root of the address works. For example if **www.mystate.gov/**greatdealcounty does not work. Just go with **www.mystate.gov**.

Fairfax County

http://www.fairfaxcounty.gov/dta/auction.htm

Botetourt County

http://botetourtbillpay.com/RealEstate/TaxSale/default.aspx

City of Lynchburg

http://www.lynchburgva.gov/property-sales-due-delinquent-taxes

City of Roanoke

http://www.roanokeva.gov/1382/Tax-Sale

Virginia Real Estate Web Sites

http://www.mls.com/search/virginia.mvc

This web site has several links to real estate in Virginia counties and individual cities right on it's landing page!

http://www.realtor.com/realestateandhomes-search/Virginia

This web site has more links to real estate in Virginia counties and individual cities right on it's landing page!

http://www.statelocalgov.net/50states-tax-authorities.cfm

http://www.brbpub.com/free-public-records/

www.RealAuction.com

www.GrantStreet.com

AVOIDING & MANAGING & ELIMINATING RISK

Legendary Real Estate investor Dave Del Dotto once said "stick with the government, they will make you rich.". Real Estate is one of the safest investments in the world, when done properly. There is risk just driving to the grocery store. The only thing separating you from a head on collision is a yellow strip of paint. That being said, there are risks in every financial investment decision you make.

Do your research. Know what you want to do, before you begin. Are you looking to flip properties? Hold on and make money on the interest rates? Are you looking for a property to live in? Are you looking to rent out properties? Each decision requires a different type of research. If you are looking to rent out properties then you need to research what the local apartment complexes and homes are renting for in the area. If you are looking to flip a property then you need to find a real estate agent that can give you comps that have sole in the area within the past year.

Visit any property you are going to bid on. You do not want to get stuck with swampland or a unbuildable lot.

AVOIDING & MANAGING & ELIMINATING RISK

You also don't want to get stuck with a property that has high property taxes. Learn the property tax rates of all the counties in Virginia or the state that you are going to invest in.

Make sure that the property has not been condemned.

Make sure that the property does not have numerous costly violations of city codes.

Ask multiple real estate agents for information on any area you are interested in investing.

Ask about possible environmental issues.

Research possible liens by builders and contractors.

Beware of a owner who may declare bankruptcy on a property. This is a manageable risk but because laws change constantly, consult a real estate attorney for more information on how to handle this risk.

Avoid scams by dealing with government employees as much as possible.

CHAPTER 3

FINANCING REAL ESTATE

8 Realistic Ways to Finance Real Estate

FINANCING REAL ESTATE

Welcome to Expert financing. I am going to show you several realistic ways to finance real estate. You are going to learn how to finance real estate with.

* VA LOANS

* PARTNERS

* INVESTMENT CLUBS

* CREDIT CARDS

* CORPORATE CREDIT

* EQUITY

* SELLER FINANCE

* HARD MONEY LENDERS

* AND FINALLY I SHOW YOU THE MONEY$!!

USING A VA LOAN

According to the web sites www.benefits.va.gov and www.military.com the current VA Loan amount is a whopping $417,000! What a lot of veterans don't know is that you can use that money to purchase not only your home, but investment properties. That is how I started my investing career. Purchasing multiple homes using my VA Loan.

FINANCING REAL ESTATE

Even if you are not a veteran, you can still partner up with one, who still has some money left on his or her VA LOAN.

If you are a Veteran, you will need to obtain a copy of your DD 214 and VA Form 26-1880 Request for a Certificate of Eligibility.

PARTNERS

This is another way I purchased a home. At the time I worked for the United States Postal Service. I had already purchased plenty of homes, so many of the workers were aware I had successfully invested in real estate. At break time I went around and ask people to partner up with me. I had multiple people offer to go in as a partner. I choose one and that house we rehabbed and flipped just two months after purchasing it. To this day it was the biggest gross profit on one deal, I have had. True I had to split it with my partner, but I would rather have half of something than all of nothing.

Having the combined resources of two people can be a great benefit, but it is not without it's challenges. If you are going to use a partner, no matter how close you are...GET EVERY THING IN WRITING.

FINANCING REAL ESTATE

Having a partner can dramatically increase the chance of a Bank lending moey as well as having someone to split the work on rehabbing, should you decide to save money and make repairs yourself. But all this must be spelled out BEFORE you enter into a Agreement/Contract and purchase a home.

It helps if the person is like minded and understands the risks and benefits of investing, and truly understands the return on investment of a particular deal.

REAL ESTATE INVESTMENT CLUBS

Real estate investment clubs are groups that meet locally and allow investors and other professionals to network and learn. They can provide extreamely useful information for both the novice and expert real estate investor. A top real estate club can provide a great forum to network, learn aboout reputable contractors, brokers, realtors, lawyers, accountants and other professionals. On the other hand, there are many real estate clubs designed to sell you. They bring in "gurus" who sell either on stage or at the back of the room, and as a result, the clubs typically profit to the tune of %50 of the sale price of the product, bootcamp, or training that is pitched.

FINANCING REAL ESTATE

I have purchased a ton of real estate books and real estate courses. Carlton Sheets, Dave Del Dotto, The Mylands, Seminar courses and much much more. I am not against any club bringing in a speaker who has a course. However I think there should be transparentcy to the members of the club.

There is certainly value in the networking that may come at one of these groups. But attend working to attain your goals and not nessicarly the a club's goal to sell you something. Some times both are the same thing. As a rule I usually leave debit cards at home the first time I attend an event. If there is a seller there with a "This day only offer" then I won't feel pressured to purchase. Plus most sellers can be convinced to sell at the offer price at a later time when you have had a chance to come down off the "sense of urgency emotional pitch" that many make.

CREDIT CARDS

When using a credit card in real estate you must really do your homework on the deal. Dan Kennedy a world famous marketer once said "always stack the numbers in your favor". That's how you use a credit card. Look at the return on investment as compared to the long term cost of using a credit card and it's interest. Also I would recommend buying low cost homes that you can purchase and own free and clear.

FINANCING REAL ESTATE

No Mortgage Payment!!! My last 2 homes I have purchased have been cash deals. One home cost $1,500 and the other about $7,000. The first was a government property from HUD and the 2nd From a Bank. These institutions are unemotional about real estate and simply view a property as a non performing asset. The 2nd home was 4 bedrooms, 1 1/2 bath and a basement located in a farming community and came with a 2 car garage/shed and .6 acre(that is the size of a NFL football field) of land.

Later in this book I will show you how to find plenty of houses with amazing below wholesale prices and a formula for almost always finding a great deal.

CORPORATE CREDIT

Many people set up corporations to buy and sell real estate as an additional protection against liabilities. Other's create a corporation to mask personal involvement in property transfers and public records. Regardless of the use of a corporation, you can buy real estate with corporate credit as an alternative to using your own cash or IRA. By capitalizing on the credit rating of your corporation, you can buy real estate and build your corporate holdings portfolio.

FINANCING REAL ESTATE

Just remember that you can set up your corporation in a state that favors you the most for your real estate deals. Do your research. Most people like Delaware and Nevada, but you will have to decide if your home state or any other state is best for you and your business.

CURRENT EQUITY

Using the equity in your home for real estate investing is another way you can finance properties. You might use the money for a down payment or it may only be enough to cover the cost of some rehab repairs.

If you stick to the low cost home formula, you may have enough to purchase the entire house. A house is an investment that should appreciate in value as well as give a great ROI (Return On Investment). Whether you decide to flip the property or rent it out for positive cashflow.

If you have equity and it's not doing anything, then you may decide to make it a "performing asset" and use it as part of your real estate finance program.

FINANCING REAL ESTATE

SELLER FINANCING

Seller finance is where the seller of a free and clear property becomes your bank along with being the seller.

Advantages:

You get to purchase the property on terms that may be more beneficial for you. Seller gets monthly payments and the benefit of treating the sale as an installment sale thus allowing them to defer any capital gains taxes that may be due.

Disadvantages:

You may be locked into a mortgage with a pre-payment penalty or may not be able to resell the property immediately. This strategy is typically not meant for flipping but can definitely be used for that purpose if structured correctly.

Because it is a known way to finance a property I have presented it in this book. But it is my least favorite because you now have a lingering relationship with your property. Your ability to make decisions regarding the property is limited and for that reason, I would don't go this route. However, like all types of financing, you have to ask yourself, "is the deal worth it."

FINANCING REAL ESTATE

I also prefer to work alone, but when a great deal came along, I sought out a partner to make it happen. Risk is usually relative to potiential profit.

HARD MONEY LENDERS

A hard money lender is usually a individual or company that lends money for investment of a secured by the investment property.

Advantages:

Less red tape the get the money. You are dealing with people who understand the real estate investment business.

Disadvantage:

This is not a long term loan. The lender wants a return on investment, usually within a few months, a a year, or a few years. The interest rate on the loan is much higher than usual conventional banks.

Using hard money has a higher risk because the return on investment is due quicker. Therefore it is good idea not to use a Hard Money Lender, until you have a great deal of experience and confidence in being able to produce a return on investment.

SHOWING YOU THE MONEY

www.businessfinance.com (4,000 sources of money!)

www.advanceamericaproperty.com

http://www.cashadvanceloan.com/

www.brookviewfinancial.com

www.commercialfundingcorp.com

www.dhlc.com
(hard money for the Texas area)

www.equity-funding.com

www.bankofamerica.com

www.carolinahardmoney.com
(for real estate investors in North and South Carolina)

www.fpfloans.com

Chapter 4

Small Business Grants

How to write a Winning Grant Proposal

Small Business Grants

Government grants. Many people either don't believe government grants exsist or they don't think they would ever be able to get government grant money.

First lets make one thing clear. Government grant money is **YOUR MONEY**. Government money comes from taxes paid by residents of this country. Depending on what state you live in, you are paying taxes on almost everything....Property tax for your house. Property tax on your car. Taxes on the things you purchase in the mall, or at the gas station. Taxes on your gasoline, the food you buy etc.

So get yourself in the frame of mind that you are not a charity case or too proud to ask for help, because billionaire companies like GM, Big Banks and most of Corporate America is not hesitating to get their share of **YOUR MONEY**!

There are over two thousand three hundred (2,300) Federal Government Assistance Programs. Some are loans but many are formula grants and project grants. To see all of the programs available go to:

http://www.CFDA.gov

WRITING A GRANT PROPOSAL

The Basic Components of a Proposal

There are eight basic components to creating a solid proposal package:

1. The proposal summary;
2. Introduction of organization;
3. The problem statement   (or needs assessment);
4. Project objectives;
5. Project methods or design;
6. Project evaluation;
7. Future funding; and
8. The project budget.

The Proposal Summary

The Proposal Summary is an outline of the project goals and objectives. Keep the Proposal Summary short and to the point. No more that 2 or 3 paragraphs. Put it at the beginning the proposal.

Introduction

The Introduction portion of your grant proposal presents you and your business as a credible applicant and organization.

Highlight the accomplishments of your organization from all sources: newspaper or online articles etc. Include a biography of key members and leaders. State the goals and philosophy of the company.

The Problem Statement

The problem statement makes clear the problem you are going to solve(maybe reduce homelessness). Make sure to use facts. State who and how those affected will benefits from solving the problem. State the exact manner in how you will solve the problem.

Project Objectives

The Project Objectives section of your grant proposal focuses on the Goals and Desired outcome.

Make sure to indentify all objectives and how you are going to reach these objectives. The more statistics you can find to support your objectives the better. Make sure to put in realistic objectives. You may be judged on how well you accomplish what you said you intended to do.

Program Methods and Design

The program methods and design section of your grant proposal is a detailed plan of action.

    What resources are going to be used.

    What staff in going to be needed.

    System developement

    Create a Flow Chart of project features.

    Explain what will be achieved.

    Try to produce evidence of what will be achieved.

    Make a diagram of program design.

Evaluation

There is product evaluation and process evaluation. The product evaluation deals with the result that relate to the project and how well the project has met it's objectives.

The process evaluation deals with how the project was conducted, how did it line up the original stated plan and the overall effectiveness of the different aspects of the plan.

Evaluations can start at anytime during the project or at the project's conclusion. It is advised to submit a evaluation design at the start of a project.

It looks better if you have collected convincing data before and during the program.

If evaluation design is not presented at the beginning that might encourage a critical review of the program design.

Future Funding

The Future Funding part of the grant proposal should have long term project planning past the grant period.

Budget

Utilities, rental equipment, staffing, salary, food, transportation, phone bills and insurance are just some of the things to include in the budget.

A well constructed budget accounts for every penny.

A complete guide for government grants is available at the website link below.

https://www.cfda.gov/downloads/CFDA.GOV_Public_User_Guide_v2.0.pdf

The guide can also be accessed at the very bottom of every page of the https://www.cfda.gov/ website.

Other sources of Government Funding

You can get General Small Business loans from the government. Go to the Small Business Administration for more information.

SBA Microloan Program

The Microloan program provides loans of up to $50,000 with the average loan being $13,000.

https://www.sba.gov/

CHAPTER 5

How To Buy a House

Strategies to Making Your Offer

Strategies To Making Offers

In microeconomics total cost (TC) describes the total economic cost of production and is made up of variable costs, which vary according to the quantity of a good produced and include inputs such as labor and raw materials, plus fixed costs.

In English... you factor in as many external costs, not just the cost of the investment property.

In order to be successful when buying investment property, you have to be good at determining the Total Cost of a property.

1. Get Investment Property Market Value

Wholesale Real Estate is real estate that is real estate priced under it's retail value. But how do you know that the retail value of real estate property? The standard formula for finding the value of real estate is to have a real estate agent find comparable (comps) properties that have sold recently. Usually about 4 properties with in a mile of the purchase property, that have sold within the past year. Formulas vary from bank to bank and real estate agent to real estate agent.

Today you can get a rough estimate by doing the research yourself. Remember that a bank will probably use their own formula, but at least you can try to get a ball park figure of a properties value by using the web sites below.

Strategies To Making Offers

Appraisal Web Sites

https://www.zillow.com/how-much-is-my-home-worth/

http://www.eppraisal.com/

2. Selecting a Real Estate Agent

So now that you have found a property, researched it's value, it's time to make an offer. As I mentioned in a earlier chapter of this book, some times you have to use a government approved agent to make an offer. Like any profession, there are good agents and not so good agents.

When I lived in Virginia, once a year the local paper published a list of all the top real estate agents for almost every real estate agent franchise/business. If your local paper does not do that then here is a formula I use for selecting a real estate agent.

Strategies To Making Offers

No part timers. Part time effort usually gets you part time results. I want an agent whose livelihood depends on their success.

Size Does Matter

The size that matters. The size or amount of properties sold. Not necessarily the gross amount of property value sold. Suppose you had a real estate agent who sold 1 million dollars worth of real estate and another who sold $500,000 worth of real estate. Which one do you choose? It depends. I want the agent who has sold the most individual properties, and not necessary the one who has the highest gross. An agent can sell only 1 house for a million dollars. The agent who sold $500,000 worth of real estate may have sold 10 $50,000 homes.

Usually a agent who makes a lot of sales has a good marketing formula in place and a good team of agents working with or for her/him. Don't be afraid to ask "who's your best agent? Why?". Often a real estate company will try to toss their worst agent a bone. Don't be that bone. Remember they work for you. Their commission comes the the property you are investing in.

Some courses teach you to negotiate the commission. I believe a proficient agent is worth the commission they desire. It's your job to select a good one.

3. "100-3" Formula

Here is a quick and easy formula for getting a great deal on a real estate investment property, using a real estate agent that you have build up some rapport with.

Have the agent find 100 properties for sale that have been on the market for at least 90 days. Have the agent fax an offer of 25% below market value to all of the properties. Because the properties has been on the market for at least 90 days, you are dealing with a more motivated seller. It is likely that 10 out of the 100 will accept your offer.

Now filter through the 10 and select the best 3 properties. Use these filters to help you select the best 3.

Strategies To Making Offers

1. What are the property taxes?

2. Are the any Homeowner Association dues?

3. What will be the appreciation value?

4. What will be your utility expenses.

5. How much will it cost, to be live in ready.

6. Is it the lowest valued house in the neighboorhood?

7. Crime Rate

Property Taxes

I once owned two homes free and clear. The homes were in the same state. Both were similar in size, but one had a $3,000 a year property tax and the other one was $300 a year in property taxes. You can guess which one I moved first. Property taxes are often overlooked, but can be a big factor in the (TC) total cost. Due your research before you make an offer.

HOA

Usually when a house seems like the perfect deal, but has been sitting on the market for a long time, look to see what the HOA dues are. Personally I stay away from any property that has HOA dues, because they can escalate and you have no control over them.

Appreciation

Look at the history of real estate apprciation. It can vary greatly form city to city, and neighborhood to neighborhood. If you are going for a quick flip then this is not that important.

Utility Expenses

The importance of the expense depends on what you are going to do with the property.

Strategies To Making Offers

Rehab Expenses

If you are not an expert, have a professional inspect the house so you can factor in, a accurate estimate of rehab expenses. Be aware of any possible code violations as well.

Cost relative to the Neighborhood

Usually it's easiest to sell the cheapest house in the most expensive neighborhood. However if you just plan on renting the house then this is not as big a factor.

Crime Rate

The crime rate can have a big impact on resale value. Use web sites like https://www.crimereports.com/ to help understand it's impact on your property.

Strategies To Making Offers

4. "Take what the defense gives you"

Take what the defense gives you is a sports metaphor for viewing the landscape of a situation and adapting to what you see.

Take a similar approach to making offers in real estate. If you tell a "For Sale By Owner" everything that is wrong with the house he or she spend a lifetime building... you may insult the owner and lose the deal.

However, you send a list of needed repairs to a HUD representative, he may reduce the price of the property, no questions asked.

Adjust your offer making strategy to the person or organization you are dealing with. The farther removed a person is from the property, the less emotional they are about making deals.

Know your profit numbers and stick to them. Especially if you are bidding on a property. Be aware of Auction fever. It will bring out the competative nature in you and can lead to you over bidding on a property.

Know your numbers and be disciplined. The reason you pick out 3 properties in the 100-3 formula is so that you have 2 other properties to go to, if your first choice does not work out.

Chapter 6

For Sale By Owner

12 Steps to Selling Any Property Fast!

FOR SALE BY OWNER
12 Steps to Selling Any Property Fast!

1. Clean and Paint the house

Make sure the house is clean and uncluttered. This makes it easier for buyer to envision themselves living there. Make the bathrooms and kitchen a priority.

2. Scent the house

You might use a light incent or place some vanilla extract and place it on a old school lightbulb to give it a fresh baked cookie smell.

3. Write a property description

Writing a great property description is key to getting buyers interested in your home. One short cut to learning how to write a good property description is to view propery listings of sold properties.

4. Take Good pictures

If you don't have a good camera, buy one. A picture is worth a 1,000 words.

FOR SALE BY OWNER

12 Steps to Selling Any Property Fast!

5. Send a email to your buyers list

If you do not have a buyer's list, here is a link to a complete set of training videos on how to build a valuable customer list.

https://goo.gl/UFSIY6

6. Post ads on craigslist

Keep reposting your ads on a daily basis so that you stay at the top of the search results.

7. **Post ads to http://www.backpage.com/**

This is a Worldwide Classified Ad Web Site.

FOR SALE BY OWNER

12 Steps to Selling Any Property Fast!

8. Place a Ad on http://realeflow.com/

This is the number one source for real estate investing leads.

9. https://www.zillow.com/rental-manager/

This is a free rental web site.

10. Create a video virtual tour

Create a video virtual tour and upload the video to YouTube. This is a powerful tool. YouTube is 2nd only to Google as the largest Search Engine in the world. However just posting a video won't get it seen. It has to be Search Engine Optimized(SEO). Below is a link to training videos that will show you step by step how to create great videos and get massive traffic viewing them!

https://goo.gl/UFSIY6

FOR SALE BY OWNER

12 Steps to Selling Any Property Fast!

11. Post an ad on facebook target a city

You can place an ad on Facebook and target the city that your property is in.

12. Place a Standard For Sale sign in the yard

If posible have flyers available as well.

13. Place addition white signs in the yard

Give more information and get more attention by placing more personal signs in the yard.

14. List propery in the MLS

If you are not a real estate agent get one to do it for you.

FOR SALE BY OWNER

12 Steps to Selling Any Property Fast!

15. Place directional signs

Help people find your house. Make sure you are not violating any county codes when placing signs.

16. Continue marketing until closing

Don't slack off. If nessicary you might want to hire VA's Virtual Assistants to keep all ads running.

17. Eliminating Negative Cash Flow

https://www.airbnb.com/

Airbnb is a web site that markets your house or rooms in your house for rent. It's easier to sell your house when it is clean, empty and buyers can envision themselves living in it.

However, if you are suffering from negative cash flow you might want to look into just renting out 1 room in the house.

FOR SALE BY OWNER

12 Steps to Selling Any Property Fast!

18. ZERO COST MARKETING

Below are a few steps to market anything using ZERO COST INTERNET MARKETING stratigies.

While there are many ways to market. In this section we are only going focuse on ZERO COST MARKETING. When you are more established you can always go for the more expensive ways of marketing after your business is producing income.

FREE WEB HOSTING

Get a free web site. You can get a free web site at weebly.com or wix.com. Or just type "free web hosting" in a google, bing or yahoo search engine.

Free web hosting is something you can use for a varitey or reasons. However many free web hosting sites add an extention to the name of your web address, and that lets everyone know you are using their services. For this reason you eventually want to scale up once you start making income.

LOW COST PAID WEB HOSTING

Free is nice, but you when you need to expand your business it is best to go with a paid web hosting service. There are several that give you good value for under $10.00 a month.

FOR SALE BY OWNER

12 Steps to Selling Any Property Fast!

19. Low Cost Paid Web Hosting

1. Yahoo small business
2. Intuit.com
3. ipage.com
4. Hostgator.com
5. Godaddy.com
6. Webhosting pad

Yahoo small business allows for unlimited web pages and is probably the best overall value, but they require a years payment up front. Intuit allows for monthly payments.

For free ecommerce on your web site, open up a Paypal account and get the HTML code for payment buttons for free. Then put those buttons on your web site.

FOR SALE BY OWNER

12 Steps to Selling Any Property Fast!

20. More Zero Cost Marketing

Step 1 zero cost internet marketing

Now that your web site is up and running you should register it with at least the top 3 search engines.

1. Google 2. Bing 3. Yahoo.

Step 2 zero cost internet marketing

Write and submit a press release. Google "free press release sites" for press release sites that will allow you to summit press releases for free. If you do not know how to write a press release go to www.fiverr.com and sub-contract the work out for only $5.00 !!!

Step 3 zero cost internet marketing

Write and submit articles to article marketing web sites like ezinearticles.com.

Step 4 zero cost internet marketing

Create and submit videos to video sharing sites like dailymotion.com or youtube.com. Make sure to include a hyperlink to your website in the description of your videos.

Step 5 zero cost internet marketing

Submit your web site to dmoz.org. This is a huge open directory that many smaller search engines go to get web sites for their database.

Chapter 7

Millionaire Rolodex

Get Started Fast with these Business Web Sites

MILLIONAIRE ROLODEX

As of the writting of this book all, of the companies below, web site is up and have an active business. From time to time companies go out of business or change their web address. So, instead of just giving you just 1 source I give you plenty to choose from.

https://goo.gl/k6DU9k

hit the link above for an instant download of this book!:

Youtube Channel Passive Income Streams Video Marketing Book:

Build an Audience

with YouTube SEO & Make Money on YouTube

Top 15 Most Popular eBizMBA Rank Real Estate Websites

Estimated Unique Monthly Visitors

1. **Zillow**   36,000,000

2. **Trulia**   23,000,000

3. **Yahoo! Homes**   20,000,000

4. **Realtor**   18,000,000

5. **Redfin**   6,000,000

6. **Homes**   5,000,000

7. **ApartmentGuide**   2,500,000

Top 15 Most Popular eBizMBA Rank Real Estate Websites

Estimated Unique Monthly Visitors

8. **Curbed**	2,000,000
9. **ReMax**	1,800,000
10. **HotPads**	1,750,000
11. **ZipRealty**	1,600,000
12. **Apartments**	1,500,000
13. **Rent**	1,400,000
14. **Auction**	1,300,000
15. **ForRent**	1,200,000

Nationwide Banks & Foreclosure Properties

Bank of America

http://foreclosures.bankofamerica.com/

Wells Fargo

https://reo.wellsfargo.com/

Ocwen Financial Corporation

http://www.ocwen.com/reo

Hubzu

http://www.hubzu.com/

Government Foreclosure Properties

Fannie Mae
The Federal National Mortgage Association

https://www.fanniemae.com/singlefamily/reo-vendors

Department of Housing and Urban Development

https://www.hudhomestore.com/Home/Index.aspx

The Federal Deposit Insurance Corporation

https://www.fdic.gov/buying/owned/

The United States Department of Agriculture

https://properties.sc.egov.usda.gov/resales/index.jsp

United States Marshals

https://www.usmarshals.gov/assets/sales.htm#real_estate

Commercial Real Estate Properties

City Feet

http://www.cityfeet.com/#

The Commercial Real Estate Listing Service

https://www.cimls.com/

Land . Net

http://www.land.net/

Loop . Net

http://www.loopnet.com/

FSBO – For Sale By Owner

By Owner

http://www.byowner.com/

For sale by owner in Canada

http://www.fsbo-bc.com/

For sale by owner Central

http://www.fsbocentral.com/

For sale by Owner: world's largest FSBO web site

http://www.forsalebyowner.com/

Ranch by owner

http://www.ranchbyowner.com/

Tools to Get You Started Video Marketing

https://www.youtube.com/

https://www.wikipedia.org/

https://screencast-o-matic.com/

http://www.openoffice.org/download/

Free Keyword Tools

https://adwords.google.com/home/tools/keyword-planner/

http://www.seocentro.com/

https://ubersuggest.io/

Promoting Your Real Estate/Videos

Top Free Press Release Websites

https://www.prlog.org

https://www.pr.com

https://www.pr-inside.com

https://www.newswire.com

https://www.OnlinePRNews.com

Social Media Websites

https://www.facebook.com

https://www.tumbler.com

https://www.pinterest.com

https://www.reddit.com

https://www.linkedin.com/

http://digg.com/

https://twitter.com

https://plus.google.com/

For Everything Under the Sun at Wholesale

http://www.liquidation.com/

COMPUTERS/Office Equipment

http://www.wtsmedia.com/

http://www.laptopplaza.com/

http://www.outletpc.com/

Computer Tool Kits

http://www.dhgate.com/wholesale/computer+repair+tools.html

http://www.aliexpress.com/wholesale/wholesale-repair-computer-tool.html

http://wholesalecomputercables.com/Computer-Repair-Tool-Kit/M/B00006OXGZ.htm

http://www.tigerdirect.com/applications/category/category_tlc.asp?CatId=47&name=Computer%20Tools

Computer Parts

http://www.laptopuniverse.com/

http://www.sabcal.com/

other

http://www.nearbyexpress.com/

http://www.commercialbargains.co

http://www.getpaid2workfromhome.com

http://www.boyerblog.com/success-tools

Small Business Resources

1. http://www.sba.gov/content/starting-green-business

2. http://www.sba.gov/content/home-based-business

3. online businesses

http://www.sba.gov/content/setting-online-business

4. self employed and independent contractors

http://www.sba.gov/content/self-employed-independent-contractors

5. minority owned businesses

http://www.sba.gov/content/minority-owned-businesses

6. veteran owned businesses

http://www.sba.gov/content/veteran-service-disabled-veteran-owned

7. woman owned businesses

http://www.sba.gov/content/women-owned-businesses

8. people with disabilities

http://www.sba.gov/content/people-with-disabilities

9. young entrepreneurs

http://www.sba.gov/content/young-entrepreneurs

CHAPTER 8
BILLIONAIRE BUSINESS ADVICE

When They Talk, We Listen.

There is a link to YouTube videos created by Evan Carmichael

Billionaire Business Advice

Bill Gates...

1. Have Energy
2. Have a Bad Influence
3. Work Hard
4. Create the Future
5. Enjoy what you do
6. Play Bridge
7. Ask for Advice
8. Pick Good People
9. Don't Procrastinate
10. Have a sense of Humor

https://goo.gl/KE5CBT

Billionaire Business Advice

Mark Zuckerberg...

1. You get what you spend your time doing
2. Get Feedback
3. Make Mistakes
4. Only hire people who you would work for
5. Make a change in the world
6. Learn from the people around you
7. Build a really good team
8. Give the very best experience
9. Care the most about it
10. Social bonds are critical

https://www.youtube.com/watch?v=HMpWXQpogqI&t=125s

Billionaire Business Advice

Oprah Winfrey...

1. Understand the next right move
2. Seize your Opportunity
3. Everyone makes mistakes
4. Work on yourself
5. Run the race as hard as you can
6. Believe
7. We are all seeking the same thing
8. Find your purpose
9. Stay grounded
10. Relax its going to be okay

https://www.youtube.com/watch?v=7a8ncSBU-Eg

Billionaire Business Advice

Michael Jordan...

1. Keep Working Hard
2. Ignite the Fire
3. Be Different
4. Fail Your Way to Success
5. Have High Expectations
6. Be Positive
7. Be who you were born to be
8. Have a vision
9. Stop Making EXCUSES
10. Practice

https://www.youtube.com/watch?v=NidqtkXq9Yg&t=8s

Billionaire Business Advice

Holy Bible...

1. Have a vision:

"And the Lord answered me, and said, Write the vision, and make it plain upon tables, that he may run that readeth it" **Habakkuk 2:2**

2. Speak Life:

Death and life are in the power of the tongue: and they that love it shall eat the fruit thereof. **Proverbs 18:21**

3. Ask for what you want

Ye lust, and have not: ye kill, and desire to have, and cannot obtain: ye fight and war, yet ye have not, because ye ask not. **James 4:2**

4. Be willing to work for it

And he shall be like a tree planted by the rivers of water, that bringeth forth his fruit in his season; his leaf also shall not wither; and whatsoever he **doeth** shall prosper. **Psalm 1:3**

Billionaire Business Advice

Holy Bible...

5. Accept Challenges

No discipline is fun while it lasts, but it seems painful at the time. Later, however, it yields the peaceful fruit of righteousness for those who have been trained by it. **Hebrews 12:11**

6. Give Back

Everyone should give whatever they have decided in their heart. They shouldn't give with hesitation or because of pressure. God loves a cheerful giver.

2 Corinthians 9:7

7. Tell the truth

But for the cowardly, the faithless, the vile, the murderers, those who commit sexual immorality, those who use drugs and cast spells, the idolaters and **all liars**—their share will be in the lake that burns with fire and sulfur. This is the second death."

Revelation 21:8

Billionaire Business Advice

Holy Bible...

8. Reinvest your profits

In that case, you should have turned my money over to the bankers so that when I returned, you could give me what belonged to me with interest.

Matthew 25:27

9. Be thankful

"Give thanks to the Lord because he is good, because his faithful love lasts forever!"

Psalm 107:1

10. Help others

The Samaritan went to him and bandaged his wounds, tending them with oil and wine. Then he placed the wounded man on his own donkey, took him to an inn, and took care of him.

Luke 10:34

Gold Medal Prayers: Brian Mahoney

https://goo.gl/GzeMAO

Please Leave a Great Review!

I have purchased all of the top real estate investing books on the market, and most have a handful of out dated web sites for their sources of properties.

There is not another real estate investing book on the market that gives you as many sources for wholesale real estate than this book.

My book gives you more and in most cases for less!

This book also gives you a web site that has over 4,000 sources of real estate financing in addition to the government's over 2,400 sources of Federal Assistance.

I have enjoyed doing all the research and sharing my real world real estate investing experience in what I hope is easy to understand terminology.

So I ask you to leave a honest and hopefully great review!

Thank you. Warm Regards,

Brian Mahoney

Get Our Video Training Program at:

(Zero Cost Internet Marketing complete 142 video series)

https://goo.gl/UFSIY6

Massive Money for Real Estate Investing

http://www.BrianSMahoney.com

Made in the USA
Middletown, DE
14 July 2025